Building Trust

HAZELDEN

About the pamphlet

When you were drinking or using other drugs you probably weren't very reliable. It will take time and effort for
you to rebuild trust with your children. This pamphlet
provides suggestions for building trust and suggestions for
striking a balance between your needs and those of your
children.

Hazelden
Center City, Minnesota 55012-0176

This pamphlet is written for parents in early recovery. If you are in treatment or have recently completed treatment and you're thinking about parenting issues, read on. The following information will help you balance your recovery needs with your parenting concerns.

In early recovery, you will have many challenges related to staying clean and sober. You may have to give up old friends or avoid places and events that might lead you back to using. You may be thinking about a job—either finding one or keeping one—so you have money for basic needs: food, clothing, housing, transportation.

The needs of your children are also important, maybe very pressing. No matter what age your children are, they have questions and feelings about your drug use, your treatment, and your role in the household now that you are in recovery.

Your children's feelings may range from anger to joy. And their feelings, thoughts, and actions may swing back and forth: they may be happy you're clean and sober at one moment but very angry for some things you did before you received treatment at the next. Those swings in mood and behavior can be very hard to predict and handle.

In this pamphlet we'll discuss four key issues that affect you as a recovering parent:

1. How your children might be feeling now that you are in recovery.
2. Balancing your needs in early recovery.
3. Basic steps to rebuilding trust.
4. Getting organized.

This pamphlet will help you understand issues that recovering parents face and will suggest ways to handle them. Why work so hard on parenting? We want you to face parenting challenges *without having to use alcohol or any other drug.* No parenting hardship should cause relapse. Using or drinking again *can only make things worse.* Remember that. If nothing else, staying clean and sober can be the strongest truth, the loudest voice you can use to tell the world and your kids "Hey! You can trust me!"

WHAT YOUR CHILDREN MAY BE FEELING

So you're no longer using alcohol or other drugs! You're probably feeling proud of yourself for going through treatment and being clean and sober now. You're probably also feeling shaky and fearful: you have to face the old problems and find new ways to handle them. We'll cover balancing your needs in the next section. Right now, let's think about your kids a moment and sort out what they may be thinking and feeling.

Your addiction has probably created several issues for your kids to think about, react to, and have feelings about.

- First, everything you did in the past while you were actively drinking or using is a history you share with them—your actions affected them.
- Second, your treatment is something they'll have feelings about.
- Third, your clean and sober role in the family might present an interesting mix of reactions from them.

How has your past behavior shaped what your kids think of you today?

Let's take a look at the past. If you were in your children's shoes, what questions and feelings would you have? Here's what they could be thinking about you and your addiction and recovery:

- Why couldn't you just quit drinking or using?
  (If you really loved me you would have quit.)
- Why did you keep drinking or using when every-thing was going wrong because of it?
  (You didn't care, were selfish, and just thought about yourself.)
- What was wrong anyway? No one ever told me any-thing except "go to your room" or "never mind, it's okay" or "it's nothing you have to worry about."
  (The adults just thought I was too stupid or unim-portant to bother telling me what was going on. They left me with a big lump in my gut and no way to understand what was happening. I didn't even know if I should worry about it.)
- Was it my fault? If I was a better kid, would you and mom/dad have fought less? Or would you have got drunk less often? or used other drugs less?
  (If I had better grades, helped around the house more, broke up your fights with mom/dad, poured

the alcohol down the drain, and so on, you would have been happier and drank or used less.)

Children think all kinds of things. They can convince themselves of anything, right or wrong, unless they have the chance to talk about what happened. What's one of the worst things that can happen to a child of any age? *To not be told what's going on.* Children know when something's happening. When that something is not named, their imaginations go wild. They have fear and anxiety instead of knowledge and understanding.

Ask your children what they think about past events. Invite them to tell you how they feel about what happened. Be careful not to turn everything they say into guilty feelings for yourself. This is about your kids. Acknowledge their experiences and feelings. It's important for you to know how *they* saw events, instead of what you remember.

Why is it so important for you to get their side of the story? Because denial is a big part of addiction. You may have convinced yourself that they didn't really know what was going on or didn't understand it. You could decide that your drinking or drug use didn't affect them. The fact is that they saw and understood a lot more than you realize. They need a chance to talk about that.

A note about guilt and shame: When you invite your children to tell their stories, the someone they are telling on is you. That's a huge risk. What parent wants to hear heartbreak in the voice of his or her own child, especially when the one who caused the unhappiness was you? Hard stuff to handle.

The purpose of getting children to talk is *to get them to talk.* The goal isn't to make you feel bad about things you did that you can't change. Make up your mind that giving them the chance to talk is more important than how you feel about what they're saying. This is meant to free both of you.

Let it happen by telling them what you hear them saying. Apologize and let it go.

What do your kids think about your treatment?
What do your children know about your treatment for
addiction? If you have spent time away from your children while you've been in treatment, how has that been
explained to them? Have you or another adult explained
where you've been? What you've been doing? Why you've
been there? And if you have been away from your children overnight, how do they feel about your absence?
Have they been afraid? Feeling secure themselves but confused about what was happening to you?

Often children are the last to know what's happening
and why. When kids aren't sure what's going on, they feel
afraid and confused. If you haven't explained treatment
to them, do it now. If you haven't told them about your
addiction, do it now. Kids understand illness, so explain
addiction by calling it a disease. You might say that it can't
be cured but can be handled, like diabetes or heart disease.
Don't hesitate to explain treatment and addiction to older
children as well as younger children, even if they pretend
they already understand it all. Many people, adults

5

included, are unclear about what addiction is, what happens in treatment, and what's supposed to happen to stay clean and sober afterward. So, whether your child is four or eighteen, explain it. Take the time.

How do your kids feel about your clean and sober role in the family?

Your recovery may stir mixed feelings in your children. They may feel anything from genuine happiness to resentment and anger. Allow for these confused feelings. When you rejoin the household as a clean and sober person, your children may feel better about the potential of returning to "normal" routines. Even if your addiction disrupted their lives, having you back may still represent security to them.

On the other hand, maybe your household has been running just fine without you for some time—before and during treatment. Then your kids may resent you. They may be thinking, *Who are you to tell me what to do or how to do it? Why should you have a say in my life? What gives you the right to suddenly be respected and obeyed as the person in charge?*

Humility is the key here. Instead of fighting these charges (which might be true), put your energy into fitting into the existing routines. Don't try to control and direct the action. Instead, figure out what the routines are and how you can help keep things flowing. If Dan and Joan eat breakfast at 7:30, dress, and catch the school bus at 8:15, you could

- fix breakfast,
- help them dress,
- wait at the corner with them.

Don't change the routine; merge with it.

Are your children used to acting as the parent or adult in the family to make up for you when you weren't taking responsibility? Many children—of any age—learn to take over when a chemically dependent parent isn't doing the job. These kids miss part of their childhood. They forget how to play, and they may be hard to win over. They are used to taking care of *you.* Now you're going to suddenly take care of *them?* they may be thinking.

Give your children lots of time to trust you again. They will have to relearn their roles, too, and that will take time. Be patient. Continue to accept and carry out your role as parent consistently. Let your children know that they don't have to carry that extra load anymore.

If your children handled decisions and proved themselves to be mature during your using days, you must respect that maturity. You need to let them make choices. You can probably trust them with decisions and give them tasks that require mature judgment. For example, your kids shouldn't have to make or enforce rules for younger siblings any longer, but they may be perfectly capable of getting younger brothers and sisters started on homework before you get home from work. Or making up the grocery list for the week. Or deciding their own weekend schedule.

Another way to build trust with kids who have played parent for a while is to play with them. These children have had to set aside play because serious problems demanded attention, sapping their energy. Now you need to create ways for them to relax and play with their friends—and with you. Playing with them may be the only way you can reach them at first.

BALANCING YOUR NEEDS IN EARLY RECOVERY

In early recovery, your first job is to stay clean and sober. If you're not clean and sober, you can't accomplish anything worthwhile as a parent.

The first thing your children will be watching for is *Are you sober?* The second thing they'll look for is *How long?* So, the first block into this bridge you're building is your recovery. Tell your kids, "Yes, I'm clean and sober today." And when all those "todays" stack up, slowly your children will let go of some of their mistrust.

Staying clean and sober comes first, so what do you need to do to build the strength of your recovery program? Let's take a moment to identify your needs. Then we'll look at simple steps you can take to balance your needs. Last, we'll set some realistic goals.

What are the key things you need to stay clean and sober? Safe housing? Connections to other recovering people? Money to tide you over until you find a job? Child care? Further counseling to help you through emotional ups and downs right now? A break in a relationship or friendship that isn't healthy?

Keep it simple. Name your top three needs and think more about those primary needs. Social service agencies can help you with basic needs like food, housing, clothing, and money. Ask a counselor to refer you to the agency that can help you begin. Take the steps to fill these needs.

You need support to keep your emotional life in balance. A group is a great place to find it. Make regular attendance in an aftercare or other recovery support group a top priority. If you need to arrange child care in order to get to your meeting, maybe you can arrange to trade off with a friend, if you can't afford to pay a babysitter. Ongoing counseling or aftercare may also help you maintain your recovery.

How will you care for your physical needs? Regular exercise can keep you healthy, minimize or prevent depression, and improve self-esteem. As a side benefit you might invite your son or daughter to exercise with you. Sometimes when communication with your kids is difficult, it's possible to find other ways to relate to them. You can build the bond without using words. Doing things together like walking, biking, running, or other physical activities can give you closeness without using words that can lead to arguments—especially when you've just begun recovery, when many subjects seem off limits.

In early recovery it's important not to try to do too much. Your most important goal right now is to simply remain on an even keel. Get enough rest, food, and exercise, and go to support group meetings. Being consistent may be the best way to rebuild trust in yourself and with other people. Be there, be consistent, keep a low profile, and do what you say you're going to do!

BASIC STEPS TO REBUILDING TRUST

Let's look at some simple steps to rebuilding the trust of your children:

- Do what you say you will.
- Be attentive, be helpful.
- Listen.
- Show up.

Do what you say

When you were using drugs, you probably weren't very reliable. You may have made and broken promises, not taken many of your kids' interests and needs very seriously, or just plain forgot about them. One thing we know for sure about addiction is that the drug comes first. That meant job, partner or spouse, finances, even kids came second or third or fourth.

For a child, inconsistency and inattention translate into one thing: *don't count on it.* Children in this situation learn to keep their guard up, ready to protect themselves in some way—whether in mind, body, or spirit.

The most meaningful way you can win their trust is by simply *doing what you say.* Over and over and over. It will take a long time for them to trust you to always follow through. They may even test you, challenge you, just to make sure you will stick to your word.

And keep it very simple. If you say you'll be home to meet them after school, be home. If you say you'll pack their lunches, pack their lunches. If you tell them you'll watch their soccer game, watch the game. Seems simple, but you know how rarely you kept simple promises when you were drinking or using. Children remember the broken promises. Your job is to lay down a new trail of promises kept. Over and over until they can rely on your word.

Be helpful

A good way to gently move back into the life of the family without upsetting its rhythms is to find ways to be helpful. This will show that you're there not to be walked on—but to offer help. Pay attention to what needs doing and be there to do it. Do the kids need a ride somewhere? Help buying school clothes? Someone to check their homework or drill them on spelling?

Some children, especially older kids, could resist or even resent your attempts to help. They may think your desire to help is meddling or interfering. Be prepared for that. Don't get angry. Instead, just back off and continue to look for ways to help.

Here's an example. After treatment, one father found that he and his teenage son simply couldn't talk to each other about anything without fighting. His son, training for track, needed someone to run alongside him and pace him. The father wanted to get in shape, so he asked to run with his son. They ran together for six months—without speaking much. One day after a long run, the son turned to his father and said, "You stuck with it." That was all that needed to be said. Slowly, they found they could talk to each other—without running!

The only opportunity this parent had was one shared interest with his son. The father found that this was a

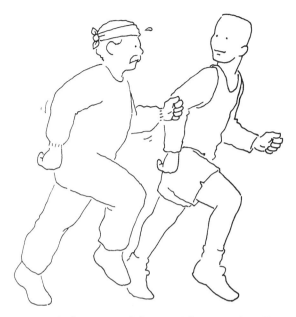

good way to help out and fit in with a routine. It took time, but it worked.

Listen

In treatment, aftercare, support group meetings, or counseling you've done a lot of one thing: talk about yourself. Talking and telling your story is part of your healthy recovery. But once home, you have another job too: to listen. Your children probably feel that you tuned them out a long time ago. The danger here is that if they don't expect you to listen anymore, they stop talking. If you've been actively drinking or using other drugs for a long time, they have a long track record of not telling you what they think, feel, worry about, or need.

You can change that by listening. Ask questions and listen to the answers. Then ask them more questions based on their answers. This is the way to let them know you really heard what they said.

Think of a time when you were talking to someone you knew wasn't listening. Remember how that felt? Didn't you feel unimportant, disregarded, even angry? Well look at the other side. If your kids felt like that over and over again, they've built up some walls to communication by now. You can't bulldoze your way through the wall, but you can work at bringing the wall down little by little by simply listening.

Show up

Just show up. Sounds easy, but a quick trip down memory lane will probably help you recall how many times you didn't. The school conferences, baseball or soccer games, pick-ups from school, rides home from the mall—the list of no-shows may be long.

And maybe you remember the times you did show up, but you were in terrible shape. Drunk or high. Remember the holidays or birthdays or basketball games when you were high? The embarrassment of those events still stick with your kids. They remember, even if you don't.

Showing up clean and sober and doing it when you say you will is another act that you need to do over and over until your kids start believing you. The beauty of this is how simple it is when you're clean and sober and in control of yourself. "What time's the hockey game? *Look for me in the stands.*" "When are you on stage for the recital? *I'll be there.*" "Will you be home at three from school today? *So will I.*" The events you show up for may not be important on the surface. What is important is just showing up.

GETTING ORGANIZED:
ORDER, ROUTINES, AND TRADITIONS

Addiction is a big disorganizer. Chances are you need basic organization in your life as much as your children do. In addition to fulfilling some of your early recovery needs, getting organized can help your children feel more secure.

Children need organization. They need order. Order, including routines and traditions, shows consistency and reliability. Order helps kids relax because they know what's going to happen. Order also helps them feel secure because they know what's expected of them. Look for ways to nurture your children through

- creating basic organization and order,
- developing routines,
- following family traditions.

Creating basic organization and order
First, let's look at getting organized. What does your household need to run smoothly? Once you have identified what you need, you can talk to a counselor or social worker for additional referrals, if your situation is unmanageable. Here are some things to look at:

1. Are your finances in order? Bills paid? Do you need to take time to work out a budget? Do you need some help doing that? A counselor can refer you for assistance.
2. Are household chores getting done? Does each family member have assigned jobs? Do you need a family "job jar" to divide up chores fairly?
3. Are family transportation needs taken care of? Are the kids ready on time to catch the school bus? Do children need rides to and from school, friends' houses, or health and dental visits?
4. Is child care taken care of? Do you need child care help for young children? Or good before- and after-school programs for elementary and high school age children? How are the kids occupied after school?
5. Do your children understand their responsibilities? Homework done right after school, before TV or play? Chores done before leaving home on Saturday

to play or do something with a friend? Pet chores done on the same day each week?

6. Do your children need medical or dental checkups? Do they need help or counseling for problems like physical or sexual abuse? addiction?
7. Do your children need help at school?

Don't make unnecessary lists of things to do. Begin to identify just what is necessary to make the household run smoothly. Concentrate on establishing enough order to do just that and nothing more. And remember, even if they resist in the beginning, children need and will eventually enjoy the order you establish.

Developing routines

Routines are activities you do on a regular basis. Taking a walk each morning with the dog is a routine. Eating breakfast at a special place on Saturday morning is a routine. Attending a church service every Sunday is a routine.

Routines are important because they give structure and organization to life. Routines make life feel more dependable, less random and full of chance. The act of doing something at a certain place and time, with the same people, can deepen and strengthen friendships. It can help you feel connected and a part of things. Routines help everyone belong. All of these benefits are as important for children as they are for their recovering parents.

Where to begin? Think of a few things you'd enjoy doing with your children—things they would like too. Think of activities you can find both the time and money for. Don't forget at-home activities like putting a puzzle together, playing some favorite board games, or renting a video the whole family wants to see. Set up a time to do that special thing and do it every week—same time, same place.

The possibilities are endless. Maybe making a batch of cookies with your children on Friday evenings would appeal to everyone. Give each child a special evening with you. Choose a day and time, and each week take that child out for a restaurant meal or movie. Walk the dog every day after work and invite a child along. Or make pizza with the kids every Friday. Once you start, routines are threads that eventually make a fabric that holds the family together. Everyone gets to belong, be loved, and relax together.

Following family traditions

Traditions are activities handed down from earlier generations and are repeated over a long time. Examples of traditions include stories passed down from one generation to the next, making certain foods, and celebrating holidays in specific ways.

The importance of honoring family traditions is in the connections we make with deeper roots—roots that go further than just our own lifetimes. Following traditions can give the whole family a sense of belonging. These ties also remind children that they are connected to something larger than themselves or their immediate family unit. That can be a very good and reassuring feeling.

What family traditions have fallen by the wayside? Talk to your older relatives and ask them how they celebrated certain holidays. Ask them for recipes or their memories of the life of the family. Explore those roots and pass them on to your own children. Routines and traditions will give you and your children a new source of strength, support, and belonging.

SUMMARY

As a recovering parent, you must balance your own needs with those of your children. If you can't stay clean and sober, you can't be a good parent. But as you do maintain your recovery, you can take simple, basic steps to build trust again with your children. It doesn't have to be complicated: just be there for them, do what you say you're going to do, and try to help out. And be patient. Trust takes time. You can succeed by taking it one day at a time.